From Faith to Action:
My Journey to Healing Communities Facing Dementia

For more Information, Visit:

www.DrFayron.com

For booking, speaking engagements, and other inquiries:

info@drfayron.com

Edited by: The Media Scientist Laboratories
Layout by: Kenisha L. Rhone
Cover Design by: Tory Brown
ISBN: 979-8-9990372-0-6

TABLE OF CONTENTS

Dedication

To the memory of my grandma, who wrapped me in unconditional love and taught me the strength of a gentle heart.

To the memory of my Aunt Bert, who instilled in me the lifelong value of education and the power of perseverance.

To my mom, my #1 supporter, whose unwavering belief in me has been a constant light.

To my Aunt Dorthy, who always kept me grounded and reminded me of what truly matters.

And to my children, whose love brings me joy even in the midst of life's storms.

Acknowledgements

As I prepare to share my journey and experience in the pages that follow, I want to emphasize the importance of acknowledging that none of us achieves success alone. I've been fortunate to have an amazing team, supportive family, numerous mentors, and influential figures who have inspired and supported me along the way.

At the forefront of my mind is Apostle Danita Jones, the senior pastor of In His Great Name Ministries (Fairburn, GA). She taught me how to communicate effectively within a male-dominated profession, particularly among pastors and other leaders. One of her tips was that you have to create a space where your suggestions become their ideas. Her guidance has been instrumental in ensuring that my messages are delivered clearly and received with the intention of inspiring action.

I must also give a heartfelt shout-out to Tonya Miller and Jacquelyn Thornton, who have been like big sisters to me. Tonya, who sadly passed away in 2020, spoke so much life into me and the work we were doing. I used to laugh at her predictions about my future, thinking they were far-fetched, which included me being on national and international media platforms. Especially, the prediction of this work reaching people outside of the U.S., which happened in 2022 with a trip to Ghana in partnership with Alzheimer's Ghana and Dr. Tiffany Washington (Associate Professor at the University of Tennessee College of Social Work). Yet, everything Tonya envisioned has come to fruition, and I am incredibly grateful for my time with her. She introduced me to Jacquelyn Thornton, President and CEO of SageNavigator, Inc. Jacque has been instrumental in my leadership development as she is overflowing with wisdom. As a Black female in the aging space, it is not easy to lead change. Jacque has been steadfast in advising me on the best approaches to navigating relationships with community organizations. She remains my family and my confidante and is my number one supporter. Jacquelyn continues to guide and encourage me, much like Tonya did, and I trust her implicitly.

Another significant influence in my journey has been Dr. Harold Koenig, the director of the Spirituality, Health, and Theology Department at Duke University. He is known for his extensive research in the fields of mental health, geriatrics, and religion. I admired his work from afar and was thrilled when he agreed to be an advisor on my faith-based home activity toolbox research project, provided I attended his workshop in North Carolina. I am glad that I agreed to those terms, as my experience at the workshop was life-changing, as it brought together like-minded individuals who were integrating their faith into their professional lives. Dr. Koenig's openness about his faith inspired me to openly embrace my own beliefs, recognizing how they influence my work and interactions. I now profess my faith to every audience before I speak. The world must understand the lens through which I am operating. At this point, I realized the intersectionality between my personal and professional journeys—what a beautiful thang.

This realization has been transformative, enabling me to help others feel comfortable on their spiritual journeys while I grow in my own spiritual journey. By being open about my faith, I've encouraged colleagues to do the same, fostering an environment where our beliefs can positively influence our work. Not everyone may accept this, and that's okay. The important thing is that this message gets to those who need to hear it, and change can happen.

I would also like to acknowledge Dr. Pernessa C. Seele of Balm in Gilead. Her work with churches and the Black community has been a significant influence on me. As a community activist, she is recognized for her efforts in establishing partnerships between public health organizations and churches to promote health and disease prevention. She has successfully engaged with policymakers, government agencies, and nonprofits, highlighting the importance of her work in eradicating health disparities. Her ability to navigate these spaces has inspired me to approach my own endeavors in a similar manner.

Lastly, I want to acknowledge my family for their unwavering support throughout my journey. No matter how far I strayed from the path, they stood by me and always showed up with love and encouragement.

Along with my family, these mentors and influencers mentioned above have played crucial roles in my success journey, and I am deeply grateful for their impact on my life and work.

Forward

Faith is a powerful concept. Hebrews 11:1, a popular passage we were all raised on in church, states, *"Now faith is the substance of things hoped for, the evidence of things not seen."* As a longtime spiritual teacher, leader, and purpose guide, I have come to know that there is something beyond faith that few get to realize in this lifetime: Divine Purpose. We are all here for a reason, and should we embrace true faith, then we know that the substance of God within us will produce evidence that we are walking our walk. There is no greater evidence I can point to for this thesis than the life—and *calling*—of Dr. Fayron Epps.

I was first introduced to her work through a mutual colleague, Mia Chester, and I was blessed with the chance to see her in action at one of Nashville's historic churches, where she was educating the congregation on the various forms of dementia that affect our community. Her energy, commitment, knowledge, and experience in her presentation were all electrifying, and I instantly knew that I was experiencing a changemaker who was on a mission.

Years later, after working with her in many capacities, I am pleased to say that she continues to be an authentic voice for healing; a voice that the fires of life experience have purified; one that has proven that hard times produce heroes, and purpose—even through pain—produces results.

In this volume, you, as a reader, will experience a behind-the-scenes look at a hero's journey. Heroes are either born or made by their circumstances. It can be argued that Dr. Epps' story is a bit of both, and the overarching result is a journey that we all can relate to: For have we not all struggled at some point in our lives with what we are on this earth to do? How many times have we seen a vision that seemed too large for us to take on, one that erased any understanding we already have that whom God calls, He will equip?

Dr. Fayron Epps, in this succinct yet powerful volume, has managed to weave together a tale of overcoming obstacles, walking in purpose, and balancing personal challenges, all resulting in creating a life-changing structure for healing the world one congregation at a time. Her humility is as powerful as her passion; truly a demonstration of putting her faith boots on the ground.

It is a story that should inspire us all—because it represents what we all can and should be doing to become the change we desire to see in the world. Church leaders will see how to effectively empathize with those they are tasked with leading; Lay leaders, community organizers, health advocates—all will learn valuable lessons on how to engage effectively with the black church; Individuals who have a dream they want to see manifest will find, in Fayron Epps, a living example for how to keep pressing on through changing circumstances.

In these pages, may you find what I have: the story of what happens when one amongst us makes the conscious decision to walk by faith and not by sight alone and, by doing so, gives us tangible evidence to prove that, while circumstances may change, purpose does not. It is the path forward for healers and changemakers, and we have Dr. Fayron to thank for clearing the way for the next generation to emerge.

Take notes in the margins, reflect on the lessons, then go and do likewise. There is no greater time than now to walk in faith.

Rev. jeff obafemi carr

Founder & Chief Spiritual Officer
The Infinity Fellowship
Nashville, Tennessee

Introduction

My name is Dr. Fayron Epps, also known as Dr. Fayron. I proudly identify as a community-engaged nurse scientist. I earned my Bachelor of Science in Nursing from Tuskegee University, a Master of Science in Nursing from Loyola University New Orleans, and a PhD in Nursing from Southern University and A&M College. I am a Fellow of the American Academy of Nursing, Southern Gerontological Society, and Gerontological Society of America.

With 25 years of experience as a nurse, as of the writing of this book, I currently serve as a Professor and the Inaugural Karen and Ronald Herrmann Distinguished Chair in Caregiving Research at the University of Texas Health Science Center San Antonio. I'm the founder of Alter, Caregiving While Black, and Engaging Beyond Dementia. These are initiatives and businesses dedicated to transforming how we care for and uplift Black families navigating their dementia journeys. I have received various accolades and funding for my innovative work in health equity, dementia care, and community engagement.

And above all, *I am a woman of God.*

At the age of 47, I can say that I am fully walking in my purpose and calling. This book is a testament to my journey of discovering my calling and creating a ministry to heal communities disproportionately affected by dementia. My ministry has been recognized for groundbreaking work in dementia care. I am dedicated to addressing health disparities within underrepresented communities where Black individuals are twice more likely than their white counterparts to experience a form of dementia. In response to this public health crisis, I founded a multidisciplinary collaborative, Alter, where I partner with Black faith communities to create dementia-friendly faith spaces. The goal of the Alter program is to improve dementia care and expand access to culturally relevant resources. I truly believe faith communities can serve as vital support systems for families and caregivers, particularly in underserved communities disproportionately affected by dementia. By combining compassion, innovation, and strategic vision, I created this dementia-friendly faith-based model for addressing health disparities in dementia care and fostering long-lasting change.

I am working to not only improve lives but also influence policy and practice in health care. My dedication to meeting communities where they are and addressing their unique needs exemplifies my commitment to meaningful change. My work has led to measurable improvements in caregiver well-being, awareness of dementia in underserved communities, and access to critical resources.

My motivation to write this book stems from my deep commitment to improving the quality of life for underserved and overlooked populations. This was inspired by personal experiences and observations of gaps in care within my family and community.

This book will highlight my journey to developing a ministry that heals communities affected by dementia. The following chapters will describe how my foundation, rooted in my faith, transformed into action.

The intention of this book is to inspire individuals and communities to lead with intention and take meaningful action.

It is my prayer that you receive these words with an open heart and that your passion is ignited, your purpose clarified, and your ministry strengthened.

PART ONE
CALLING

Chapter 1

How it All Began

My journey to spreading dementia awareness and healing communities didn't start with me creating the Alter program (a dementia-friendly congregational program), and it certainly didn't begin with the goal of doing it well. It developed organically in response to the community's needs.

When I set forth to do this work, my goal was to educate the Black community. I didn't choose to start with the church, but the community chose to begin with the church. In other words, the church chose me. To make this happen, I asked faith leaders and churches to open their doors, allowing me to provide education to their parishioners and the broader community. That's where it all started. The overwhelming response that I received, not just from the community and parishioners but also from the faith leaders, ignited my spark to say, "Oh, I may be really in a space where we can do something meaningful!" This may be a space where I can establish formal partnerships with churches, helping families currently facing dementia and preparing those who are not. So, not just asking them to open their doors so I can do education but genuinely partnering for success. Fast forward, and these partnerships have led to a movement!

As far as the official "spark" moment goes, I always return to my Bishop, Bishop Glenn B. Allen Sr. of Destiny Christian Center International (Fayetteville, GA). He called me to his office and asked me to come up with a way to serve the church, which led to providing dementia education in the church. However, it was another Bishop, Bishop Aaron B. Lackey Sr. of the Temple of Prayer Family Worship Cathedral (Fairburn, GA), who challenged me and my team to think about how to take this education to the next level. Bishop Lackey asked, "What do you want me to do with this education?"

I did not have a response for him.

I shared this encounter with the team, and we agreed, "Yes, we have to give them [faith leaders] something." Initially, we developed an algorithm to guide the next steps if you notice signs and symptoms of dementia in yourself or someone else. Then my colleague, Dr. Theodore Johnson (Professor at Emory University School of Medicine), met with me and said, "Hey, I want you to be part of this project related to the geriatric workforce and focus on dementia; please come up with something." That moment marked a significant opportunity for my work, and now faith leaders and parishioners from all over the world are being recognized as part of the geriatric workforce, affirming the need for my work.

As a nurse scholar-activist with a PhD, I also know through research that there is a desperate need to create learning and supportive environments for families, many of whom attend church somewhere. Opportunities to receive dementia educational programming existed; however, they were not reaching the Black community. I receive comments and praises on a regular basis from faith leaders and parishioners for not overlooking them as so many do. I just wonder how anyone can overlook a community and not take any action to help them when they are being hit the hardest by dementia. At times during my journey, I have felt that I was all over the place, just living from moment to moment. But now I know that this feeling was my work evolving organically to serve God's people. While on this journey, there was also this growing, burning internal drive to make a way out of no way. I wanted to be a part of a solution.

As I reflect on my journey. I remember all the problems being shared by the community. I also remember what Bishop Lackey asked and what Bishop Allen said: *"God told me to call you and for you to get involved in a ministry."*

And, of course, I laughed at his statement. What ministry would I start? I responded to him by saying, "I don't do kids, so I can't help out in the Youth department. I don't sing, so I can't join the music ministry. I don't get to church early enough, so I can't be an usher or greeter." He then asked, "What *do* you do?" I told him that "I do older adults and dementia." He inquired more about dementia because he wasn't familiar with it. Then he said the words that put the wheels in motion:

"Start a ministry around what you do."

I laughed even harder because I had just moved to Atlanta within the last year. How could I dare dive headfirst into the local landscape? I know Churches in any given city are a tight community. However, if I am honest and fast-forward to today and look back, it was truly God working through him—and he listened. If he had not listened to God's voice, so many families would have gone without help, and so many faith communities would not have been transformed.

Praise God for obedience.

From Faith to Action

Before moving to Atlanta, I was living in southeast Louisiana, where I partnered with the local chapter of the Alzheimer's Association. Even then, I was involved in education within the church. The spark must have always been there, lying dormant, poised for my awakening and activation on a much larger, more challenging level.

As an educator, nurse, and community advocate, I was always open and willing to help and support the community and churches. I just never had anyone challenge me to say, "start a ministry." I am, first and foremost, a woman of faith, and I always lean on the church for support and guidance. I grew up seeing my mother, a single mother of three, rely heavily on the church for so many things. All I needed was someone to trust and challenge me. I needed someone to say, Hey, you need to do that. The fire sparked and spread like wildflowers afterward. I just needed someone to spark it, to put me on that path, to challenge me.

I know it was all God's doing, given how things lined up. This is how I can tell you that tapping into what you are here to do, your purpose, will make a difference not just in your life, but in the lives of others. I am not going to pretend that the road has been easy because that's just not true. But it was easy—in a sense—once I listened to God. I have become a different person on this journey. As I listened and understood that my assignment was to serve His people, through this work, using the skills, gifts, and talents He gave me. I hold several degrees and have hands-on experience working in various hospital settings. He gave me these experiences and skills. Once I realized, "Oh, this is my assignment," everything fell into place afterward. So, even when people shut the doors in my face or didn't answer my phone calls, I didn't see that as a failure, but rather as just part of this journey. Once I embraced my purpose and calling, everything changed. I was able to see God's favor upon my life.

I had to let Fayron go and let God.

When you are on assignment, you don't give up. I stayed persistent because I knew that this was my Purpose, that which I was called to do.

Chapter 2

More Than My Circumstances

I describe my life during the time I was called out to start a ministry by Bishop Allen as a "hot mess." At least, I felt that it was. I was divorced and a single parent of three, with one child being for a married man. I had been to jail just a few years before moving to Atlanta. I was broke, lonely, lost, and my nursing license was on probation. I now laugh when I think about when Bishop Allen called me into his office. It was a warm day in September, but I was dressed as if it were a cold day in January. Every part of my body was covered in clothing! I was wearing a tan hat, a long-sleeved jean shirt, brown winter boots, and camouflage long pants. Metaphorically, I didn't want him to "see my sins." All you could see were my eyes. Again, I didn't know why he was calling me into his office, and I didn't want him to see this imperfect human being who was feeling defeated and lost.

I had a lot going on in my life. I was running away. Well, I thought I was running away from my past and especially my life in Louisiana, and with everything that I had going on, I was truly lost. I was confused, and I couldn't understand why he was calling me into his office.

I felt that I didn't honestly know what I was doing in Atlanta. I just didn't know. I knew I needed to do something different from what I did when I was in Louisiana. I am in a new city, raising my kids as a single parent with no village, trying to figure this out and navigate this new world. I didn't have a lot of money either, so at this point, I am just trying to make it, not disappoint my family, and not have to depend on anyone.

Yes, I had a lot going on, to say the least, but isn't that true for all of us? We all have a lot going on and "life be life-ing." Even in the midst of it all, however, I accepted the challenge presented by Bishop Allen to start a ministry. I reflected and realized that I had done it before, when I returned to school to obtain my doctoral degree under similar circumstances. Even then, it was a case of someone challenging me by saying, "God told me to call you."

My PhD journey began after I dropped out of school, as I was exhausted from "hard" living. I listened back then to a professor, Dr. Sharon Hutchinson (former chair of the graduate nursing program at Southern University and A&M College), whom I never met, but she said, "God told me to call you and tell you to get your butt back in school." I listened, went back to school, and I was able to finish my PhD—in just one year from the day she placed the call to me. That was all God.

When Bishop Allen said those words, I immediately thought back to that PhD moment, and my spirit said, *"Listen, my child."*

From then on, I didn't have to "sell" or beg for anything. There were people in my life whom God was using, whom he had planted beforehand. I had no clue of their purpose in my life until I accepted this Calling and my purpose. These individuals were those I met through my first research project in Atlanta, which involved conducting a culturally informed community health assessment. Usually, when this happens, you meet people, get information, and move on. But God was planting seeds months before I accepted his calling on my life, by meeting people through my research and developing relationships with them. The people he planted in my life became my family, my village, and they joined me on this mission to serve his people and create dementia care systems in Black churches. God is so amazing!

When I prepare to speak to people, I always pray, "Order my steps, God, order my steps," and He indeed has done just that. I ask Him to do this every day so that I can fulfill my assignment and do it with love. While I don't seek fame, some people from my past might be surprised at what I have been able to accomplish in life. Others might laugh because I have been known to be "slow" in grasping concepts. I feel good, though, because when it's all said and done, I am here, with Him, existing in—and because of—His light.

While I am still becoming the person that he called me to be, I can confidently say that I realize that this is a spiritual journey for me. It's not just about me bringing people and faith communities together for healing, creating a movement, and organizing and educating the Black church. It is truly a Spiritual Journey, my Spiritual Journey.

I thank God for my foundation—my faith.

I recently went to dinner with a friend, and they pointed out all the accolades I have received for my work and how people now reach out to me to partner for change. She asked me how I stay so humble with all of this going on, how I never let it all get in the way of me just being "regular Fayron." I immediately thought back to that fashion trend of the '90s when people wore the bracelets "WWJD" *(What Would Jesus Do?).*

That was my response. I shared with her that it's the way I operate, in fact the only way to operate.

What would Jesus do? In every situation I find myself in, I ask myself what would He do? I believe He gave us the path, the book, a guide. I want to ensure that I am using it to approach everything. So, even in conflicts, what would He do? When I'm introducing a new program to a community, what would He do? How would He introduce this?

I try my best to stay in that spirit. I think as long as I'm in that spirit, I can make things happen. Things will change, and things will move. I am changing outcomes for my community, equipping churches, and helping individuals on their own Spiritual Journeys.

Ultimately, I hope to serve as a witness to what God can do when we say yes.

Y'all, I wasn't running from life; I was running toward God's blessings.

Chapter 3

The Journey into The Unknown

When I first embarked on my journey to educate churches about dementia, it wasn't about organizing them into a network. My goal was to promote dementia awareness, particularly within the Black community, which often didn't realize the extent to which dementia affected us. Growing up, I believed dementia disorders, such as Alzheimer's disease, primarily affected white people. Even as a PhD-prepared nurse, I held this misconception, unaware of anyone in my family with a diagnosis. This lack of awareness was prevalent among my family and community, and I knew it needed to change. I decided to start my outreach and education to churches because they are the cornerstone and haven of many communities.

As a woman of faith, it only made sense to me to start my outreach efforts in the church, allowing me to integrate my professional and personal life. Pieces of the puzzle were all coming together for His good–A beautiful thing!

I began this journey in Louisiana during my postdoctoral studies, volunteering for the Alzheimer's Association and speaking at churches. I lived in the suburbs of New Orleans area during this time (2013-2015), and I was interviewing Black families affected by dementia and educating the community when families and the community were still trying to "bounce back" from Hurricane Katrina. This was very challenging, but I knew I had to hear from these families, educate, and bring resources to the community. I could not stop because dementia does not stop. This experience set the foundation for my next steps. and gave me the comfort and confidence needed to continue this work when I moved to Georgia.

In 2016, I moved to Georgia. Upon arriving in Georgia, I was advised to start my research and community outreach efforts in churches, given their prominence in the community. It was crucial to ensure that both church leaders and congregants had access to the necessary information.

Starting this work (now recognized as my *ministry*) in Georgia came with challenges. Initially, I didn't know where to begin, but I was determined. Through my research, I connected with wonderful people who joined my community advisory board, supported my mission, and helped with outreach to the community. These individuals became my team, my family.

Pastor Martin Jakes, Sr., who was a neighbor of one of the advisory board members, opened their church, Light of the World International (East Point, GA), to us, marking the beginning of our outreach in the Atlanta metropolitan area. The first events had low attendance, but we persevered. Over time, our efforts paid off, and we began to see packed rooms.

Another challenge was gaining access to more churches. Initially, only my church in Fayetteville, Georgia, and Pastor Jakes' church in East Point, Georgia, opened their doors to the community. But by sharing the mission with colleagues, family, and friends, more churches began to invite us. Our efforts required time and dedication, often necessitating the sacrifice of personal time to achieve our goals. We attended faith alliance and church meetings repeatedly until people started listening. As awareness grew, more people became personally affected by dementia, increasing their interest in our work.

Working with predominantly male pastors was another hurdle. A female pastor, Apostle Danita Jones, the senior pastor of In His Great Name Ministries (Fairburn, GA) mentored me on how to communicate effectively with male leaders. Her guidance was invaluable in breaking down barriers and ensuring my message was heard.

Persistence was key. By remaining steadfast and committed to our mission, we overcame all obstacles.

When engaging with faith communities, I presented information in a relatable manner, fostering a knowledge exchange rather than a one-sided lecture. This approach made our ministry successful.

In November 2019, the Southern Christian Leadership Foundation in Tuskegee, Alabama, invited me to speak. It was a full-circle moment, as I had studied at the Tuskegee University. During this event, someone remarked that I had started a movement. Initially, I didn't understand, but over time, I came to realize the impact of my work. This is a movement!

By 2025, this ministry has grown significantly, with partnerships in multiple states and over one hundred faith partners. Reflecting on this journey, I see parallels with the civil rights movement, which also began with a single idea and grew through the support of its community.

Throughout this journey, my relationship with God has deepened. I've learned to listen to His guidance, which has been instrumental in our success. In conclusion, this journey has been about more than just raising awareness about dementia. It's about building a movement, empowering communities, and fostering change. I'm grateful for the mentors and influencers who have shaped my path and look forward to what lies ahead.

Chapter 4

Navigating and Managing Conflict

Navigating conflict often involves addressing differing goals and interests among individuals or groups. I have always been able to navigate conflict with ease. I have never been in a physical fight because I am not easily defensive, and I try to understand the other party's viewpoint.

I recall when my family was struggling to make ends meet and I had to get on food stamps. Well, as a result of not reporting a new source of income in a timely manner, I was arrested. The conflict came when I was placed in a jail cell with over 20 women, and I was aggressively approached by one of the cell "bullies." This could have turned out badly, but I leaned on my nursing skills and communicated with my cellmate using SBAR (**S**-Situation, **B**-Background, **A**-Assessment, **R**-Recommendation; a technique used to facilitate prompt and appropriate communication in health care settings). I recognized that she was hurting and just wanted to be seen and heard. Within 10 minutes, I had diffused the situation and began teaching my cellmates about the importance of feminine health.

After posting bond and reflecting on this experience, I realized that one of my gifts was conflict management. Recognizing this as a gift, I have been able to bravely face difficult situations in my personal life and turn them into positive circumstances where everyone walks away understanding the appropriate next steps to take that will benefit them.

In my experience with dementia awareness outreach to the Black community, I've found that conflict is relatively rare. The community's shared understanding of the disadvantages it faces and the work I'm doing to address these issues and disparities generally fosters unity rather than discord. People are often excited to see someone taking initiative and bringing new ideas to the table, which helps minimize conflict.

However, questions do arise, such as why my focus is primarily on the Black community. Recently, someone questioned why my research programs focus solely on Black individuals and families. I explained that my goal is to create safe environments for Black caregivers and individuals living with dementia to learn and thrive. I recognize that Black families are hit the hardest by health disparities and are often overlooked and don't have access to supportive programs and services. My work is designed to promote quality of life for Black families affected by dementia through meaningful engagement. This focus is not about exclusion but about inclusion and addressing specific needs within the community.

While I haven't faced significant conflict within the community, I have encountered challenges within my team. Conflict is inevitable in any professional setting, and I consider myself skilled in conflict management. I strive to create an open environment where parties can express their viewpoints and understand each other's perspectives. By facilitating these conversations, conflicts often resolve themselves as individuals recognize the pros and cons of their actions and decisions.

The real challenge I've faced is navigating the politics within churches. I was unprepared for the complexity of church governance, which often involves multiple layers, such as congregations, office staff, ministry leaders, and executive committees! These structures can create bottlenecks, making it difficult to reach decision-makers, such as senior pastors. I've learned that faith leaders don't always hold the final say, and navigating these layers requires patience and understanding.

One situation involved addressing disrespectful behavior from a church leader towards a team member. This incident threatened to undermine my team's morale and spiritual growth. I addressed the issue directly with the leader, emphasizing the importance of maintaining a spirit of respect and kindness in all business interactions. The leader eventually apologized, and I used the opportunity to remind my team of the importance of staying focused on our mission, despite challenges.

Overall, while I haven't faced significant conflict within the community, managing team dynamics and navigating church politics have been ongoing challenges. These experiences have taught me the importance of patience, open communication, and maintaining focus on our mission to serve and empower the Black community.

Chapter 5

Defining Success

Reflecting on what success looks like in educating churches and the community about dementia, I find it challenging to define it in a single way. Initially, I developed a logic model with my team outlining steps to obtain goals such as enhancing empathy within the Black community, increasing knowledge about dementia, promoting memory screenings, and encouraging early detection. These are measurable outcomes we strive for, but success is more nuanced than just metrics.

For me, success is found in the individual stories and testimonies of those we've helped. Each time I hear about a family benefiting from resources and supportive programs at the churches we've partnered with, or a pastor who now knows how to support a caregiver in their congregation effectively, that's success. It's not about the number of individuals, families, and communities reached; it's about the impact on each individual, family, and community.

One story that stands out is when a pastor shared that a new member, who was a caregiver for her mother with dementia, felt comfortable bringing her mother to church because the pastor had spoken about dementia from the pulpit.

I had another pastor call me on my cell phone and say that he needed me to help one of his parishioners (a member of a prominent Black political family in the U.S.) who confided in him about their family experience with dementia. He was glad they called him, and he had a source to give them. This daughter graciously received the resources and guidance that I provided to her. If this pastor had not felt comfortable sharing resources, this family would not have received the help they needed. They did not have another outlet that they trusted. This is what success looks like to me.

Witnessing church leaders and congregations taking the lead in implementing dementia programming to meet the needs of their members warms my heart. Before this initiative, many pastors were unaware of how to support families dealing with dementia. Now, they are equipped to reconnect these families with their spiritual communities, providing much-needed support. This work is about more than just education; it's about reconnecting people to a significant part of their lives and ensuring churches are prepared to support them.

While I can provide numbers and metrics, true success is seen in the changed behaviors and the new support systems that have been established. This ministry is dedicated to creating a welcoming environment where families can share their journeys and receive support.

Together, we are creating dementia care systems in Black churches.

Chapter 6

Adapting and Creating
Community Solutions

We all need to be prepared to adapt to change. To stay relevant, we must recognize and respond to the changes occurring around us. In today's rapidly evolving social and political landscape, adapting our engagement strategies is crucial.

Reflecting on the pre- and post-COVID era, it's clear that staying relevant requires recognizing and responding to the changes around us. When COVID-19 hit, I had just launched a dementia-friendly congregational program (Alter) with churches, having been in full swing for about two years. Initially, I thought the pandemic would derail my team's efforts, but a colleague encouraged me to see it as an opportunity to reevaluate, pivot, and reimagine.

Despite the pandemic, the needs of dementia-affected families and faith communities remained. The team shifted program delivery to online platforms and developed programming tailored to the pandemic's challenges, including vaccine education and addressing social isolation. This pivot led to increased interest from churches, aligning with the mission of the Alter program. The pandemic, while challenging, also revealed new opportunities and ways of thinking.

Regarding the current political climate, I have faced questions about whether my work continues to focus on the Black community, given that dementia affects everyone. Early on, I struggled with this, but my team and advisory board constantly reminded me of our mission: to empower the historically disadvantaged Black community.

Moving to Texas, where the Black community is a minority, brought new challenges. As I engaged with faith communities, I considered expanding our program to the Mexican-American community. However, the San Antonio older Black community urged me to prioritize their needs, emphasizing the importance of having something built by and for them. This again reinforced our commitment to serving the Black community first.

When invited to speak at a council meeting in Washington D.C., I faced pressure to demonstrate how our program could serve diverse communities. I shared our story and offered our framework as a model for others, while maintaining our focus on the Black community. This approach was well-received, enabling us to assist others without compromising our mission.

While the Alter program primarily serves Black congregations, we also share resources and consult with others. We are here to help non-Black families and communities, but they must be willing to do the work with us. However, I must say that, regardless of who we share resources with, our focus remains on shining a light on the Black community, ensuring they are not overlooked.

I am committed to serving and healing our communities, ensuring they know they are seen, heard, and supported. I won't follow mainstream trends or chase funding. I want Black families affected by dementia to receive the quality services and support they deserve.

I've come to realize that this work cannot be done as a solo act. It takes a village—a collective effort—to create meaningful change and have a lasting impact, truly. We need to come together to support every Black family facing dementia and work towards reducing risks for those not yet affected. We can no longer wait for others to create treatments and solutions for us. As a community, we have the knowledge and power to serve our community and address dementia-related disparities. We must hold each other accountable and support one another.

Community only exists to the extent that everyone can adapt and participate in it. For those seeking inspiration on being a true change agent for healing, it's all about ensuring people take action.

Dr. Bashir Easter, Founder of Melanin Minded LLC, once said at our first Alter Dementia Summit in 2024 that "the solution is within us." This resonated deeply with me. By bringing the Black community together, we can create our own solutions and support systems. We live in these communities, face these challenges, and have the power to find solutions. Together as a community, we can combat this disease and promote quality of life.

When we come together as a community, we can accomplish great things. Reflecting on my journey, I realize that bringing people together has been key to this movement and creating our own solutions. Who better to address the challenges we face than those of us living in these communities? We've encountered numerous obstacles throughout our lives, but we also hold the solutions within us. Together, we can support families, combat diseases, and promote quality of life.

That's what it's all about.

Despite the political climate and geographic location, I will continue to advocate for the Black community. My work remains dedicated to the Black community, committed to providing the quality services and support they deserve. Despite external pressures, I will continue to advocate for Black families affected by dementia, ensuring they know they can depend on me. While I offer to share our principles with other communities, the work requires their active participation. Until then, I will proudly serve the Black community, driven by love and a commitment to healing and empowerment.

I'm grateful to be in a position where I can utilize my education and skills to help others, guided by my faith and my passion for the community.

Chapter 7

Integrating Personal and Professional Life

Throughout my career, the concept of work-life balance has been a constant topic of discussion. It's a challenge that resonates deeply with the work I do, especially in grassroots efforts and community activism. For those of us immersed in these fields, balance often feels like a distant dream. How can you achieve balance when you're living and working within the community you're striving to uplift? When I lived in Atlanta, I chose to reside on the south side, in predominantly Black communities, because it was important for me to face the same challenges as those I was advocating for.

In this context, balance becomes elusive. Even mundane tasks like grocery shopping are tinged with awareness—I'm not just buying groceries; I'm evaluating the quality of produce and thinking about food accessibility. The idea of cutting off work from personal life seems impossible. Then, I encountered the term "work-life integration," and it resonated with me. It felt like a revelation, a way to embrace my commitment to activism without feeling like I was failing at achieving balance.

This integration enables me to continue my work, particularly in the realm of dementia activism, where change is desperately needed. My children, too, have been part of this journey. As a single parent, I've integrated them into my activism, bringing them to events and exposing them to the importance of community work. It's not always easy, but it's essential for them to understand the value of leading and caring for others.

Many ask how are you doing all of this community outreach and raising three children as a single parent? With the support of my children and community, I have made it "do what it do." That means, conducting virtual presentations during volleyball and baseball games or while waiting for my daughter at dance practice. I have also had church members pick up my kids from practice so I can extend my time teaching the congregation. By any means necessary to spread the word and reach the people.

With my children integrated in my activism, they know their mom is all about helping people, knew their mom was helping people and they started spreading the word. For example, my son heard his baseball coach talking about his mom with dementia and he sent the coach directly to me for help. My son also has joined the Alter youth council, created an Instagram account for caregiver self-care, and written school papers on dementia.

Work-life integration also extends to my team. We blend work with leisure, like going bowling or skating after meetings. This approach is vital for my survival in this field. People often ask how I take care of myself, and while I engage in self-care activities, the work itself is fulfilling. Helping others and sharing stories fuels me, even though there are moments of exhaustion.

The weight of the community's burdens can be heavy, and I often wonder how past leaders like Martin Luther King, Jr., and Malcolm X managed to keep going. It's not burnout, but the sheer weight of responsibility that can be overwhelming. Self-care becomes challenging when the burdens of the community are ever-present.

I also relate to pastors who carry the weight of their congregations, and this understanding helps in my conversations with faith leaders. We strive for better self-care, recognizing that we must take care of ourselves to continue serving others effectively. I don't have all the answers, but I'm committed to finding ways to relieve this weight and engage in meaningful self-care.

Passing the burden to others isn't a solution, as I don't want them to carry heavy shoulders either. Instead, I focus on work-life integration, continuing to advocate for the community, my peers, and my family. The work may not yield immediate results, but every small victory is significant.

For those in similar positions, don't let societal expectations of balance make you feel like you're failing. Embrace what works for you. For me, it's work-life integration, where my personal and professional lives intersect seamlessly. I find strength in my faith and community, knowing that the work we do is not in vain.

We are making a difference, and together, we will continue to push for change.

PART TWO
COMMUNITY

Chapter 8

Inspired by their Voices

Throughout my journey over the past decade, I've been inspired by the voices and stories of the community. These voices have been instrumental in shaping my path and reinforcing my commitment to the work I do. One of the most impactful moments occurred during my visit to the Southern Christian Leadership Foundation in Tuskegee, Alabama. It was Professor Dr. Lonnie Hannon who first told me, "You are leading a movement." At the time, I didn't fully grasp the significance of his words, but now I see the truth in them. This realization has been echoed by many, including my sister, Barbara Epps, who recently attended one of my presentations and affirmed, "This is a movement, sis."

Another voice that has stayed with me is that of Reverend David Hamm, President of the General Missionary Baptist Convention of Georgia District 3. He expressed gratitude, saying, "Thank you for seeing us." His words highlighted the importance of prioritizing the

Black community, which has often been overlooked and left with the remnants of resources. This acknowledgment has strengthened my efforts to prioritize addressing the needs of my community, recognizing the years of neglect and the necessity for consistent support and infrastructure.

Pastor Martin Jakes, Sr., from Light of the World Church International (East Point, GA) also offered valuable insight early on in my journey. He reminded me that not every faith leader would join this movement, but those who do are the ones meant to be part of this journey. This understanding has helped me manage expectations and focus on collaborating with those who share the vision of healing and transforming our community.

The voices of my children, my biggest cheerleaders, have also been a source of motivation. My oldest son (21 y.o.) and daughter (19 y.o.), who have witnessed my journey from uncertainty to purpose, express pride in my work. Their support reminds me that my efforts are not only shaping the present but also creating a legacy for the future.

In addition to community activism, my work has unexpectedly led me to guide others on their spiritual journeys. Students and team members have shared how their involvement in this work has inspired them to explore their spirituality. This aspect of my work, though unplanned, has become an integral part of my mission.

I've been described as a connector, someone who facilitates access to resources and opportunities. This role is something I embrace wholeheartedly, as it aligns with my lifelong commitment to helping others achieve their goals. Being approachable and down-to-earth has been both a personal trait and a professional asset, enabling me to connect with people from diverse backgrounds.

Despite initial critiques of my speaking style, I've learned to embrace my authentic self. My journey from a child in speech therapy to a confident speaker has taught me the value of authenticity. I am proud of who I am and the path I've taken, and I remain committed to being true to myself and my community.

In summary, the voices of the community, my family, and my own experiences have shaped my journey and reinforced my commitment to leading a movement that addresses the needs of the Black community. Through collaboration, authenticity, and a focus on healing, I aim to create lasting change and inspire others to join this important work to heal our communities facing dementia.

Chapter 9

The Future of Health Education
in The Black Church

The Black church has long been a cornerstone of the community, playing a crucial role in advancing health education and initiatives. Public health professionals and other experts have historically partnered with Black churches to address various health issues, recognizing the church's influence and reach within the community. One notable example is Dr. Pernessa Seele's work with the Balm in Gilead, which focused on raising awareness about HIV by collaborating with Black churches. This partnership model has been documented as an effective way to engage the community and promote health education.

However, the future of health education in the Black church involves going beyond traditional methods. While providing education seminars and raising awareness are important, it is equally crucial to equip faith leaders with the necessary tools and resources to respond effectively to health challenges.

This approach empowers churches to take action and ensures the sustainability of health initiatives. By empowering faith leaders, we can create long-term, lasting impacts on community health.

To achieve this, it is essential to stay informed about the specific needs and challenges faced by each community. This requires understanding the unique priorities and disparities present in different regions and tailoring health initiatives accordingly. By remaining relevant and responsive to the community's needs, we can ensure that our efforts resonate and have a meaningful impact.

In my community outreach to churches, the ultimate goal is for faith leaders to take an active role in advancing health agendas. Ideally, they would reach out to health professionals and experts, recognizing the disparities in their communities and seeking collaboration to address them. While this is already happening to some extent, there is a desire to see more faith leaders initiating these partnerships and taking proactive steps to improve the health and well-being of their congregations.

In summary, the future of health education in the Black church involves empowering faith leaders, providing them with the necessary tools and resources, and fostering collaboration between churches and health professionals. By advancing a health agenda and equipping churches to respond effectively to health challenges, we can create a healthier, more resilient community.

Chapter 10

The Role of Technology

When I first embarked on writing this book, the significance of technology wasn't immediately apparent to me. However, as I delved deeper into my journey, I realized that technology has played a crucial role in my life and work in serving and healing the community.

When the COVID-19 pandemic struck, forcing many communities into quarantine, we had to adapt quickly. My team explored platforms such as Free Conference Call, Zoom, and Microsoft Teams to continue our outreach work uninterrupted. This technological shift allowed our work to expand beyond the Atlanta metro area, reaching other states and broadening our impact.

Upon reflection, technology has played a crucial role in our growth. It enabled us to extend our community activism, connecting with more churches, faith leaders, caregivers, and individuals in need of support. Through video conferencing platforms, we taught churches how to enhance their worship services with technology, providing them with the necessary resources and tools. This expansion ensured that more people felt seen, heard, and supported.

With faith communities now online, I can participate in various services through social media platforms. Although attending every worship service in person is impossible, technology allows me to engage with multiple services, leaving messages and interacting with the community.

This connectivity has been invaluable, helping me maintain relationships and stay informed about community activities.

Living in Texas while my team is spread across Georgia, Alabama, Minnesota, Virginia, and Mississippi, technology has become essential for our team's communication as well. Video conferencing and social media platforms have been particularly effective, enabling us to share messages and stay informed about community developments. Our presence online keeps communities engaged and motivated, as they know we are actively involved. In summary, technology has become an integral part of our operations, facilitating communication and expansion.

Initially envisioning our reach within one state, five years later, the Alter program is now present in over 20 states, thanks to the resources and opportunities technology has provided. By embracing these tools and allowing divine guidance to shape our path, we have reached countless families, fulfilling our mission in ways that far exceed our initial expectations.

Chapter 11

Sustaining Momentum

When embarking on a new initiative or movement, it's crucial to understand from the outset that this is a long-term commitment. Initially, I didn't foresee my work with faith communities as a long-term endeavor. I thought it would be short-term, but as the journey unfolded, I realized the need for a committed team and strategies that would sustain momentum.

These strategies weren't pre-planned; they evolved as the movement grew. Now, as I look forward to the next five to ten years, I would like to share some lessons learned from the past five years.

To sustain momentum, it's essential to start strong and finish strong. Often, people fail to recognize the need for strategies to maintain energy and enthusiasm throughout a project, resulting in a weak finish. It's vital for leaders and visionaries to maintain momentum so that the project reaches its full potential and continues to transform, meeting the needs of the communities it serves.

Here are **six key strategies** for sustaining momentum, applicable to both your team and the community:

1. Pour into Your Team and Community. Encourage and uplift your team and community throughout the process. Just as you face challenges leading the initiative, they face challenges supporting it. Feed their spirit and be there to uplift them.

2. Listen Actively. Truly listen to your team and community, not just to hear them but to respond meaningfully. When people feel listened to and recognized, they are more motivated to continue contributing.

3. Identify Strengths and Weaknesses. Understand the strengths and weaknesses of your team members and build on their strengths. This reduces pressure and enables individuals to excel in areas where they are skilled and enjoy themselves.

4. Align with Long-term Goals. Discover the long-term goals of your team and community. Show them how their participation in the initiative aligns with their goals, creating excitement and commitment.

5. Celebrate Successes. Take time to celebrate achievements, no matter how small. Recognize the hard work of your team and community and let them know their efforts are appreciated.

6. Transfer Ownership. Train team members to take on leadership roles, giving them a sense of ownership and responsibility. Encourage communities to identify leaders who can co-lead initiatives, ensuring sustainability.

These strategies have helped sustain momentum over the years, keeping my core team engaged and attracting new members. While managing a larger group presents challenges, it also allows for greater reach and impact.

Ultimately, sustaining momentum ensures that initiatives have a lasting impact, reaching more families and individuals and serving God's people effectively.

A Note on celebrating Even the Small Wins

From my perspective, there is no such thing as a small victory. Every win, every accomplishment—whether personal, professional, or within the community—is significant and impactful. The work I am doing in the Black community and within our churches is making a real difference, and each success, no matter the size, deserves to be celebrated as a major achievement.

For instance, when a Bishop reached out to me about a parishioner in need, it was a victory on multiple levels. First, it showed that the Bishop recognized the resources available to support his parishioners.

Second, the fact that the parishioner felt comfortable enough to share her caregiving journey with her Bishop, who had spoken about dementia from the pulpit, was another significant win. It demonstrated the growing awareness and willingness of faith leaders to address dementia openly, which has been a challenging journey.

These moments, where faith leaders and community members reach out for support, are not just small steps; they are monumental strides in building trust and establishing a network of care. Trust, especially with faith leaders, is not easily earned, and I do not take it lightly. Each call, each connection, and each story shared is a testament to the impact we are making. Celebrating these victories is not about public recognition or accolades. For me, it's about giving praise to God for allowing me to use my gifts to serve His people. Our celebrations are rooted in gratitude and worship, acknowledging the divine guidance and favor that enable us to continue this work. By doing so, we ensure that our steps are ordered, and our efforts are blessed, allowing us to make a difference, truly.

Reflecting on my journey, every goal achieved and every lightbulb moment for a parishioner is a cause for celebration. I celebrate daily, and my celebration is a form of praise and worship, recognizing that without divine support, none of this would be possible. There is no victory too small to be celebrated, and each one is a testament to the progress I am making along with my team to empower our communities.

Chapter 12

Enhancing Empathy

A good general definition of empathy is *the ability to understand and share feelings with others or to experience the feelings of others*. So, if you examine that definition, it is not straightforward. People are not born with this sense, but you have to lead by example.

Therefore, if you want others to develop or enhance an individual's empathy in a particular situation or topic, you must lead by example. I take that seriously. I carry out my life in a way that allows me to think about others and understand what they may be going through, which helps me better serve them and be there for them.

My nursing background, having been a registered nurse since 2000, has really helped with the empathy aspect. I'm working with a multidisciplinary team, so they are not nurses per se, and their education doesn't focus on that aspect.

It's up to me to be able to lead by example and to share with them how to connect with the person that they're serving, how to communicate with our communities that we are serving, understand what they may be going through because that is so needed for us to be able to serve them and provide them what they need.

Again, as a nurse, I've had years of reflection after each shift I worked, trying to think about the patients I cared for that day. Because sometimes on the floor, you're just so busy and you're going, going, going, but it's so crucial for me to take a minute to reflect on my day, reflect on those that I care for, what was going on in their life. How are they feeling now with this diagnosis, now having to change their daily regimen, and how will their illness affect their livelihood and family?

When I returned to the unit the next day, I felt I had more empathy for my patients. So, yes, I had several tasks to do, but now I approached them in a different spirit because I took the time to understand what they may be going through and how I could better support them in that situation.

When I was working in hospital settings, I was also in leadership positions. In these leadership positions, you work with a large staff that comes from diverse educational backgrounds, and they may not grasp it immediately, because not everyone in healthcare shares this spirit of empathy.

You, again, have to lead by example.

I recall one situation where it was over the weekend, and I came in on Monday, but it was my weekend staff that I had to bring in for a meeting. My reason for bringing this to a meeting is that I received a letter from a family member complaining about the care of their mother over the weekend. Specifically, they mentioned that their mother had been given spoiled milk and that the mattress did not have air in it.

She was on a special air mattress bed, but there was no air in the mattress, and everyone just had excuses. Their mother stayed there in that bed over the weekend, and I received a complaint. The patient had a stage one bed sore, which can develop into a serious issue. And so, of course, I was upset. And, as I spoke with the staff, they didn't see that there was anything wrong.

Right there, that's when I challenged them. I didn't know what to call the feeling; I didn't know it was "empathy" at the time, but I needed them to see what it was like to be in that patient's and family's shoes; What were they going through?

So, I called a meeting and shared the situation. Then, at the end, I said, 'What if that was your grandmother?' I made it really personal to them, and that's when I saw the light bulbs go off again when I challenged them, and I said, "What if that was your grandmother? Would you want your grandmother to lie on a mattress with no air on it? Would you want your grandmother to be fed expired milk?"

Again, light bulbs went off, and this was me making a personal connection with them. For them to relate to this, it's about putting themselves in that person's shoes, not just being patient, but also considering the family members of that patient.

And that hit home.

With my community outreach work, it becomes more challenging. I am trying to enhance empathy within the community for individuals living with dementia and their caregivers. Each family is unique, and actions can be misinterpreted, leading to judgment, stigma, and anger.

For example, we once had a situation with a family caregiver and a person living with dementia. This family caregiver was speaking harshly to their spouse who was living with dementia, and that can be taken the wrong way by someone from the outside, appearing to be abusive.

However, if you don't sit there and truly observe, taking the time to speak with the caregiver and understand why they may need to communicate in this way, you won't grasp it.

So, I had to sit there, take it in, and speak to the caregiver so I could understand. They were open to explaining their reasoning on why they talk harshly because of the type of dementia their spouse had. So, that was me now gaining empathy for the caregiver in their role.

I then had to share that with a member of my team so they can fully understand that everyone is different. Every family dealing with dementia is unique; every caregiver is distinct; every care partner is unique. So, you can't just say, 'Oh, yeah, I have empathy.' This is ongoing. This is something I'm not sure whether to call a characteristic or a trait, but it's something that requires ongoing effort.

When I go out into the community and speak, I share the stories of families that I've encountered through my research projects and community outreach. And that has really helped open their eyes and enhance their empathy.

Storytelling enables people to step into the shoes of those affected by dementia or other conditions. As before, when I share that story, it's really good to allow them to see it in a true storytelling format that is truly engaging.

Another method we've used in our community education is role play. Being able to have our audience engage in role-play or watch a short skit helps them understand what it's like to be in someone else's shoes or experience another person's feelings, particularly in the work I do, which involves dementia.

There are various ways to enhance empathy, but its role is extremely important. That's actually one of our goals for the Alter program.

The work that I do with the churches through the Alter program enhances empathy. I am trying to reduce dementia-related stigma. And by doing that, people have to truly take the time to understand what it's like being that other person, to understand their feelings and what they may be going through and reflect on that.

When you enhance empathy, you're able to serve at a whole different level. I was able to recognize that when I was providing acute care in a hospital. So again, what's so important is taking the time to reflect and then seeing how you can change what you're doing and adjust your approach. Now, when you interact with that family caregiver, family, or person, you'll be interacting with a different understanding.

I had one member of the community who was the pastor's wife, engage in a virtual dementia simulation exercise. This is when you set the stage with props for participants to engage in activities that simulate living with dementia. We did this with her, and at the end, she said, "I'm going to go home to see my mom. I'm going to look at her with new eyes."

She had tears in her eyes when she shared this feedback. This is what empathy looks–and feels–like.

Chapter 13

Advice for Engaging the Black Church

When considering building bridges with the Black church for successful community initiatives, the first question to ask yourself is, "What is my why?" Understanding your motivation is crucial. Is it driven by a genuine desire to improve health outcomes and uplift the community, or is it simply about securing a grant? If your motivation is purely financial, your efforts may not yield the desired results. The community will see through insincerity, and money alone cannot compensate for the dedication required—long hours, frequent communication, and the patience to explain new initiatives.

Passion is essential. It fuels the extra effort needed to make a difference. Your work should be driven by a genuine commitment to the community, not personal recognition. Remember, the focus should be on highlighting the community's achievements, not your own.

Respect is paramount. To work effectively with the Black church, it is essential to respect its history and its role within the community. This requires an understanding and appreciation of the church's significance and the faith leader's role. Take the time to learn about the church's history and its impact on the community.

Patience is key. Building trust and implementing programs takes time. Don't expect immediate adoption of your initiatives. Do your homework, be persistent, and remain consistent in your actions.

Familiarity with faith practices is important, but you don't need to be an expert in every denomination. Your role is to master your community initiative, not the church's doctrine. Ask questions and engage in informal conversations with church members and leaders to learn from them. This will help you introduce and implement your program in a way that resonates with the community.

Be comfortable with your own spiritual journey. Know where you stand in your faith, as leaders may inquire about it. It's okay to be honest about your journey, whether you're deeply involved in church or just beginning to explore your faith.

To establish a successful partnership, consider these **seven key steps**:

1. Understand the Culture and Community. Learn the history and role of the church or organization within the community. Understand what matters to the people it serves.

2. Identify Key Contacts. Identify the touchpoint person or point of contact who can assist you in sharing your work and its significance.

3. Evaluate the Opportunity. Assess whether the partnership is a good fit and whether the community has the necessary infrastructure to support the initiative.

4. Design Your Program. Clearly define the pillars of your program and how it will be implemented within the community.

5. Consider Sustainability. Plan for the long-term sustainability of the program within the community.

6. Implement and Activate. Once you've done your homework and designed the program, work with the community to implement it.

7. Measure and Monitor Impact. Conduct program evaluations, surveys, and gather data to understand the impact of your initiative.

By following these steps, you can join me in creating a culture of care while leading meaningful change within the community and building lasting partnerships with the Black church.

Chapter 14

Legacy and Impact

When I reflect on the legacy I hope to leave behind, I envision a narrative centered around fearless leadership and unwavering commitment to community empowerment. I want people to remember Dr. Fayron Epps as a trailblazer who dared to step outside the conventional boundaries set by society and the healthcare profession.

My journey with the Alter program is a testament to this, as it was born from a desire to serve the community and address unmet needs, particularly within the Black church.

I hope to be remembered as a nurse-scientist who was unapologetically vocal about her faith, integrating it into her professional endeavors. This aspect of my identity has been pivotal in my success, demonstrating that faith and professional life can coexist and even enhance one another. By collaborating with faith leaders, I have demonstrated how programs can be effectively implemented to ensure long-term impact in the community and sustainability.

The work with the Black church is a significant part of my legacy. It represents a unique initiative that experienced rapid growth and success, not because of any one individual, but because of a collective effort. I have always strived to include everyone in this journey, fostering a spirit of humility and collaboration. I want to be remembered for making everyone feel seen and heard, for listening intently, and for responding with empathy and action.

Moreover, I hope to be recognized for my ability to connect with people from all walks of life, from community members to senior pastors, and for my commitment to making information relatable and accessible. My approach has always been to lead by example, embodying the principles I teach and living a life that others can look to for inspiration. I also want to be remembered for my willingness to challenge the status quo, to think outside the box, and to encourage others to do the same.

My journey has been about showing that there are alternative paths to success, paths that do not necessarily align with traditional academic or professional norms. I have been intentional about being authentic and consistent, ensuring that my interactions with others are genuine and transparent.

Ultimately, my legacy is about the movement I have led with Black faith communities, a movement that has equipped faith leaders with the tools they need to effect change in their communities. It is about improving the quality of life for families affected by dementia and ensuring that they receive the support and resources they deserve. I want to be remembered as someone who was unapologetic in her dedication to empowering and healing the Black community and who inspired others to follow their passions and make a difference in their own unique ways.

IN CONCLUSION

Over the past decade, my journey has been marked by significant personal growth, particularly in the last five years. Although I've been involved in the dementia field for about 10 or 11 years, it's during these recent years that I've truly evolved as an individual, a mother, and a leader. This transformation is largely attributed to my work with faith communities. Engaging directly with faith and ministry leaders has been an invaluable experience. While I provide them with information to support their congregations, they, in turn, minister to me, offering life lessons and spiritual guidance that have profoundly impacted my personal development.

I never imagined that I would find myself quoting Bible scriptures or relating my life experiences to spiritual teachings. This spiritual growth has not only influenced me but also members of my team, some of whom began without a strong faith background. Witnessing their spiritual journeys has been incredibly rewarding. As I continue to grow, I look forward to the future, knowing that much of my personal development is owed to my engagement with faith communities through the Alter program.

Every interaction with faith leaders feels like a worship service, where I receive messages that I actively apply to my life. This growth extends to my role as a mother. Balancing my dedication to community work with parenting has been challenging, but my faith has strengthened me as a parent. The skills I've developed through my programming work have translated into my personal life, enhancing my patience and resilience.

I am grateful for the lessons and messages I gain from each interaction with faith communities. These experiences have enriched my personal relationships and provided me with a network of spiritual advisors who offer support and resources without me even asking. This reciprocal relationship is invaluable, as I pour into them by equipping them to serve their communities, and they, in turn, equip me for everyday life.

Reflecting on my journey, I see the influence of my mother, aunts, and grandmother in myself. Their wisdom and strength inspire me, and I am proud to carry their legacy forward. I now feel comfortable offering counsel to others, a role I would have shied away from five years ago. This confidence is a testament to the work I've done with faith communities and their impact on me.

As a leader, I've always had a natural ability to galvanize and guide others. My experiences in academia and community work have honed these leadership skills. Working with faith communities has placed me in diverse spaces where I've had to elevate my game, especially as a Black female nurse. These experiences have enriched my leadership abilities and allowed me to uplift others.

Throughout this journey, I've gained confidence in myself as an individual, mother, and leader. I trust my ability to make appropriate decisions for various situations and stand by them. This confidence, coupled with the recognition of my growth by others, is truly a cause for celebration.

For myself, and now hopefully for you, we get to bear witness to what it means to transform faith into action.

FAYRON EPPS, known affectionately as Dr. Fayron, is a highly recognized and lauded for her groundbreaking work in dementia care and dedication to addressing health disparities within underrepresented communities. Her focus on integrating faith-based organizations into dementia care is not only innovative but also deeply impactful, as it leverages trusted community structures to provide support and education.

Her efforts to create dementia-friendly faith spaces and educate caregivers demonstrate a profound understanding of the cultural and emotional dynamics that influence caregiving in African American communities. Moreover, her research reflects compassion and a commitment to equity, qualities that are crucial in healthcare and academia.

RESOURCES

Below is a partial list of dementia and caregiving-related resources recommended for exploration:

The Alter Program
Equips faith communities with practical tools and resources needed to support their parishioners and community members affected by dementia.
https://alterdementia.com/

Engaging Beyond Dementia
Provides activities that nourish the spirits of families affected by dementia. They offer the Beyond Box, which is a treasure trove of activities that intertwine faith, community, and cognitive stimulation.
https://engagingbeyonddementia.com/

Boss Frog
Educates the youth about common illnesses and diseases that are crucial components in fostering empathy, understanding, and support within families and communities.
https://www.bossfrog.org/about

Respite for All Foundation
Creates engaging, volunteer-based respite programs for churches and community agencies.
https://respiteforall.org/

Melanin Minded
Provides information, service, and support for people of color with a long-term vision to empower and equip people of color to have the optimal quality of life. They have a special focus on youth and dementia capable transportation services.
https://www.melaninmindedllc.com/

Alzheimer's Association
Offers resources, support groups, educational material, and information about Alzheimer's and other dementias.
https://www.alz.org/

Alzheimer's Research and Prevention Foundation
Provides information on holistic approaches to maximizing brain health.
https://alzheimersprevention.org/

AARP
Offers resources and support for caregivers. They also have an online program to help individuals build healthy habits to promote brain health, Staying Sharp.
www.aarp.org

Roon
Provides access to insights from leading physicians and people with lived experience to guide individuals with both expertise and real-world understanding.
https://www.roon.com/

Best Programs for Caregiving
Provides a free online directory of proven support programs for family and friend caregivers of individuals living with dementia.
https://bpc.caregiver.org/

Savvy Caregiver
Offers training programs to help family caregivers face Alzheimer's disease and other dementias.
https://savvycaregiver.com/

National Council of Dementia Minds
Ensures that people with dementia have a powerful voice in both personal and public conversations. They have a special group dedicated to Black/African American individuals living with dementia, Black Dementia Minds.
https://dementiaminds.org/

The Association for Frontotemporal Dementia
Provides information on improving the quality of life of individuals affected by Frontotemporal Dementia.
www.theaftd.org

Lewy Body Dementia Association
Raises awareness and provides support for individuals and families affected by Lewy Body Dementia.
www.lbda.org

Positive Approach to Care
Offers a series of simple techniques focused on practical dementia care skills. Their approach is based on understanding the areas of the brain that are no longer working and making use of the parts of the brain that are still active.
https://teepasnow.com/

Lorenzo's House
Empowers young people and their families walking with younger-onset dementia through an array of holistic support, shifting the narrative from isolation to connection, stigma to strength, and darkness to light.
http://lorenzoshouse.org

Hilarity for Charity
Supports families affected by Alzheimer's disease through advocacy, education, and caregiver support.
https://wearehfc.org/

BrainGuide
Offers a platform that empowers people with knowledge and resources to take the best next steps in managing their own or a loved one's brain health.
https://mybrainguide.org/

Clinical Trials-TrialMatch
Provides information on the importance of participating in clinical trials. As part of this education, they offer TrialMatch, which connects individuals living with cognitive impairment, Alzheimer's disease, or another dementia, caregivers, and healthy participants with current research studies.
https://www.alz.org/alzheimers-dementia/research-and-progress/clinical-trials

Clinical Trial Connector
Offers a free, confidential tool that helps patients, caregivers, and clinicians find suitable Alzheimer's trials.
https://mybrainguide.org/clinical-trials/

NOTES:

From Faith to Action

www.ingramcontent.com/pod-product-compliance
Lightning Source LLC
Chambersburg PA
CBHW031227120626
46545CB00003B/1026